REPORT WRITING

by
Roger Lewis, National Extension College, Cambridge
and John Inglis, Barmulloch College, Glasgow

D1340189

The National Extension College,
18 Brooklands Avenue, Cambridge CB2 2HN
© National Extension College Trust Ltd. 1982
ISBN 0 86082 320 2

The National Extension College is an adult teaching body providing education through correspondence courses, publishing, tapes, slides and kits, weekend study sessions and day seminars. As a non-profit making company, registered as a charity, all monies received by NEC are used to extend and improve the range of services provided.

National Extension College correspondence units are a range of self-tuition texts designed for use by adult students. These texts are suitable both for use by home-based and college based students. Colleges interested in materials for class use should write to the Course Texts Department for a catalogue of materials available.

Written 1982 by John Inglis and Roger Lewis.
Designed by Peter Hall.
Printed by NEC Print.

CONTENTS

How to use this book

This is not just a textbook telling you what to do. As well as giving you advice we give you plenty of chances to practise and to get comments on your practice. We have written this introduction to help you learn from this book and to use it to the full, and it is essential that you read it before moving on to Chapter One.

At the beginning of each chapter you will find a list of what you should be able to do by the time you get to the end of that chapter. You can use this list in two ways:

- to prepare yourself for what is to come
- to check back, at the end of the chapter, to ask yourself how well you have learnt each skill

(We put a box by each point so you can put a tick if you feel you have successfully mastered that skill.)

We give you the chance to test yourself on each skill in two ways. Firstly, in the **SAQs** (short for 'self assessment questions'). You should try these every time and not read what follows until you have spent time working at your own answer and writing it down on a notepad.

Then, when you have put the effort in first, you can read on and compare your answer with that of the authors. You get a second chance to measure your progress in the questions at the end of each chapter, in the **Check Your Learning** sections. You should answer these in just the same way as the SAQs — that is, write down your points and *only then* look at the answers the authors give.

There are also **Activities** in the text. These are things you can go and do, using the skills you have developed. Many of the activities ask you to look at examples of reports. You can get these from a library or from your file at work. The Activities also relate to the actual reports you yourself may be writing at the time when you are studying this text. (If you are not writing a report then you should follow the advice on selecting a topic given below to writers of Assignments.) If you are working in a college then you can show your work on these Activities to a member of staff or another student; if you are in business or industry then you may find a training officer or manager helpful. If you are entirely on your own then why not ask a friend or a member of your family to take a look at what you have written to see if it makes sense? You can also use the Activities to check any reports you may write in the future.

If you are working through the course with a tutor (provided by your college, your firm or by NEC) then you will need to write answers to the **Assignments**. Assignments B to E should preferably be answered for a report you are currently working on. It may be, however, that you have no report to write at the time of studying this book. If that is the case then you should

either think of a topic from your work or studies on which you might be asked to write a report.
or choose one of the topics listed below.

(If you decide on the first alternative make sure that your tutor agrees with your choice.)

Topics for Assignments
- An elderly aunt of yours wants to buy a new, economical motor car. Which car should she buy? (You will have to provide information about her needs.)
- A friend is coming to live in your neighbourhood and is working in your own firm. Advise the friend on the best way of getting to work (and back).
- You are moving house. You investigate the houses in a particular area (price, conditions, etc.). Write a report to guide your own decisions about which kind of house to buy.
- You are applying for a job. You are asked to write a report on your career so far. This report will accompany your application.

Your tutor's comments (which you should always wait for before sending off your next Assignment) will help you to relate this course to your own circumstances. Similarly, if you are studying in industry your training officer or other representative of your firm may ask you to complete some or all of the Assignments.

In the last Assignment we ask you to write a complete report based on your work earlier in the course. Although reports vary greatly in their length depending on their subject matter and scope, for the purposes of this course you should aim to write a final report with a minimum of 600 words and a maximum of 1800 (between two and six sides of average handwriting on A4 paper).

The City and Guilds of London Institute examination, which is specially for students of this course, consists of two parts:

● Coursework assessment, based on Assignments B to E
● A written examination, set by the City and Guilds of London Institute

Further details of the examination will be sent to you on submission of your first Assignment. If you wish to take this certificate it is essential that you have a tutor.

We also hope that you will enjoy using this book and that it will help you with your report writing.

We hope that you will return to this book many times after you have studied it. It is intended for flexible use, as and when you need help. You will find some skills easier to master than others. Certain aspects of your report writing will need further attention and you can return, as and when you want, to particular sections of the book.

Now test yourself on this introduction by answering the Check Your Learning questions, and then move on the Chapter One: What is a Report?

CHECK YOUR LEARNING

1. (a) What is the purpose of the Check Your Learning questions?
   (b) What is the purpose of the Activities?

2. How do Assignments differ from Activities?

3. 'To work through the book once will put right any problems you have with writing reports.' Is this true or false?

Answers to Check Your Learning

1. (a) To give you a second chance to measure your progress.
   (b) To enable you to try out your new skills 'for real'.

2. You hand, or send, Assignments to your tutor for comment.

3. The statement will, for most people, be false. Rarely can all problems be put right at one stroke. You are more likely to have to return to particular parts of the book for further practice.

CHAPTER ONE

What is a report?

After you have worked through this chapter you should be able to:

● **list the main features of a simple report** ☐

● **give reasons for these features** ☐

Reports are written for a variety of reasons. School or progress reports give information on the performance of an individual or department; a surveyor's report helps you to decide whether or not to buy a house; a *Which?* report shows which stereo unit or car is good value. Reports often lead to action; they help people to take decisions.

SAQ 1_____

What decisions may be taken as a result of reading

- *a school report on a 10-year old*
  on a 17-year old
- *a* Which? *report?*

As with all SAQs, write down your answer before you read on.

School report
In the case of the 10-year old child it would probably be the parents who would read the report. They may decide to reward the child in some way for good performance or to arrange extra tuition if the child needed it. The

17-year old would be more involved in taking decisions him or herself, e.g. to work harder at French.

Which? report
Reading this may lead a reader to buy one brand rather than another, or, perhaps, to decide not to buy that particular product at all.

So reports are usually written to help people take decisions about real-life issues. Readers of reports want to get quickly to the main points. They expect to find conclusions clearly stated, and information provided to help them to take their decision. Reports thus have to be written in a way that helps readers quickly to find the answers to the particular questions they are asking. A very simple report will have a format such as:

● Title
● Introduction
● Main body
● Conclusion

As we shall see later, longer reports may contain other sections as well, such as appendices or a summary.

SAQ 2_____

Name the parts of a simple report.

_____

Title
Introduction
Main body
Conclusion

The following are two versions of a brief report prepared by the Housing Committee on a proposed development of houses on Footsway Meadows.

10

SAQ 3

Read both versions. Then say which you think is the better version. Give reasons for your answer using the discussion earlier in this chapter of what makes a good report.

(a)

REPORT

The Housing Committee has had three meetings to discuss this matter and a number of reports have been received from the Borough Surveyor and the Legal Department.

Our Legal Department reports that there are no restrictions, i.e. no rights of any kind and no encumbrances that would prevent building. But the site does have some problems. It is a triangular block and this would mean that those houses built close to the apex will have much smaller gardens than those on the other side. We understand too that a few of the contractors in the town are not busy and we should expect some competitive tenders.

Consequently we suggest that the Council should proceed to find out what grants will be available, what the cost of building would be by taking some provisional tenders.

The site does seem to be suitable for building and all the indications are that it would take two- or three-storey houses. We have been informed by the water, gas and electricity authorities that these services are all readily available. We would recommend that the Council proceeds and decides to build here because we have heard that private developers are interested in the site.

(b)

PROPOSED HOUSING ON FOOTSWAY MEADOWS

INTRODUCTION

The Housing Committee has been asked to report to the Council on whether or not an estate should be built on Footsway Meadows.

The Committee has had three meetings to discuss this matter and a number of reports have been received from the Borough Surveyor and the Legal Department.

LEGAL CONSIDERATIONS

Our Legal Department reports that there are no restrictions, i.e. no rights of any kind and no encumbrances that would prevent building.

(b) is much more clearly organised. It achieves this in the following ways:

• by a title
• by headings. There is an introduction and a conclusion (both essential features of a report) and two central parts could be said to make up the 'main body'.
• by the way material is grouped. In (a) the conclusion is split between the third and fourth paragraphs instead of being gathered together as in (b). You will notice other places where (b) groups material more logically than (a).
• (b) states clearly who has been asked to write the report and why. The report is also signed, so it is clear exactly who is responsible for it.

The most immediate and striking difference between (a) and (b) is the clear headings (b) gives. These 'signpost' the reader to the relevant points. The busy executive, council member or academic hasn't time to waste. He wants to go straight to the sections that concern him (often the introduction and the conclusion). Few reports are read right through, word for word. The busy reader will expect to find certain kinds of information in certain places; if he doesn't find what he expects then he is quite likely to lose confidence in the person who has written the report.

There are other good reasons for disciplining yourself to write within the report framework:

- It helps you to remain *relevant*. If you force yourself to write a *title* and to state your purpose in the introduction then you are far less likely to wander off the point — and wandering off the point is all too tempting!
- It helps you to improve all your writing, not only of reports but also of essays, notes, memos, minutes, letters and any other kind of written work you have to produce.
- to be forced to classify information into particular sections is very good mental training.

SAQ 4

Go back over the previous section. Four advantages are given of using a strict format for your reports. List them briefly (one line to each).

It helps busy readers to find what they want
It helps the writer to stay relevant
It helps the writer to produce more effective written work — in whatever form
It is good mental training.

ACTIVITY 1

Find some examples of short reports (e.g. in your local library or at your place of work). How are they divided up?

CHECK YOUR LEARNING

1. Which of the following statements are accurate?

(a) Reports are always 500 words long
(b) Reports help a specific reader to take a decision
(c) Reports are written in a tight structure

2. Fill in the blanks to indicate the main features of a simple report.

   T . . . .

   I . . . .

   M . . . . b . . . .

   C . . . .

3. Give *two* reasons for following the report format set out in the unit.

Answers to Check Your Learning
1. (b) and (c) are correct. (a) is not necessarily true. Some reports (such as those published by governments) are very long indeed, running to hundreds of pages; others are very short. There is no standard length.

2. Title
   Introduction
   Main body
   Conclusion

3. See the answer to SAQ 4.

ASSIGNMENT A

This assignment asks you to provide information on *your own* report writing. Your answers will help your tutor to advise you on how best to tackle the course and, if you wish to, on whether or not to enter for the City and Guilds Certificate in Report Writing.

● How often do you write reports?
  (or How often do you expect to have to write reports?)
● For whom do you/will you write them?
● For what purposes?
● How long are they/will they be?

- What is the nature of the organisation you work for?
  (or, if a student, What course are you on?)
- What main problems do you have when writing reports?
  (or do you expect to have?)
- How do you hope this course will help you?
- What do you think so far of this course and the way it is set out?

Terms of reference, titles and introductions

After you have worked through this chapter you should be able to:

- list three elements making up the 'terms of reference' of a report ☐
- say why the terms of reference are so important ☐
- know when to ask for the terms of reference to be made clearer ☐
- write an effective title ☐
- write an effective introduction ☐

What are 'terms of reference'?

'Terms of reference' is rather a vague phrase. What does it mean? Well, the *Concise Oxford Dictionary* defines it as follows: 'points referred to an individual or body of persons for decision or report, (definition of) scope of inquiry, etc.' We could unpack this to include

- the subject matter of the report
- the purpose of the report
- the reader or readers of the report.

Let's look at some examples.

Read the following extract from a memo:

> Look into the reasons why the Thorn 450K machine has so many faults, particularly breaking threads . . . Prepare a report for the Managing Director.

SAQ 1

Write down (a) the subject matter of the above report
(b) the purpose of the report
(c) the reader for whom the report is to be prepared

(a) The subject matter is the Thorn 450K machine.
(b) The purpose is to 'look into the reasons why the Thorn 450K machine has so many faults, particularly breaking threads'.
(c) The reader is the Managing Director.

The Office Manager says to his secretary:

> We badly need some new typing chairs. Go down to the supplies and have a look at what they've got . . . don't make cheapness the main consideration . . . we want good chairs but we don't want to pay too much. Report before you put in the final order.

SAQ 2

(a) Who is to be the reader of this report?
(b) What is the subject matter?
(c) Briefly, and in your own words, say what the purpose of the report is. Check your answer back against the terms of reference.

(a) The Office Manager
(b) Typing chairs
(c) Information that leads to the purchase of suitable chairs.

Notice that you need to define the subject matter closely. In the first example the report should not be a general discussion of the 450K machine but a report on why it has so many faults and *particularly* the fault of breaking threads. Taken together, purpose and reader help you to decide how to handle the subject matter. Terms of reference are thus vital: they tell you *what* the report is to discuss, *why* it's needed and *who* will read it.

Look back to SAQ 1. What follows is the opening of a report written to meet the terms of reference given there.

THREAD BREAKAGE IN SEWING MACHINES

INTRODUCTION

Thread breakage in sewing machines is a serious problem which can cause a good deal of frustration among seamstresses who are on piecework and also causes delays in production. Sewing machines all tend to have this problem but some experience it more than others.

THE SEWING STATION

I spent some time working in the sewing station which has several of the most modern Viscount machines and they seem to be fairly free from the problem of breakage...

and so on...

SAQ 3_____

Does this opening succeed in satisfying the given terms of reference? Read it carefully and check back to the purpose of the report as stated in the answer to SAQ 1. Give reasons for your view before you read on.

No, it's not really successful. The terms of reference ask the writer quite specifically to consider *the Thorn 450K machine.* Yet this machine is not even mentioned. The title shows that, right from the start, the writer is treating the topic too generally (*all* sewing machines rather than the Thorn 450K). Admittedly, thread breakage is considered and the Thorn machine may be implied by the phrase 'some experience it more than others'. But this is not direct enough, and the relevance of the writer's experience of the sewing station is not made clear.

In this example the writer of the report is to blame: the terms of reference were clear and he is ignoring them. But sometimes terms of reference are vague and before you can meet them you need further information. Here is an example:

The Office Manager is rushing out to attend an important meeting. As he leaves he shouts over his shoulder to the Chief Clerk who has just been appointed to the firm

SAQ 4———————————————————————————————————————

If you were Mrs Stevens, what would you want to know?

I should need to know more about the *purpose* of the report. The subject matter is clear enough — office equipment — but what aspects of it should Mrs Stevens consider: the condition of the equipment? What equipment needs replacing? The cost of new equipment? Developments in technology or design? And who is to *read* the report: the Office Manager himself? a committee?

The title

We'll assume that the terms of reference are clear, i.e. that you know the subject matter, the purpose and the reader. The next stage is to decide on a title for the report. It's a good idea to restate in your own words the terms of reference. You have already done this in SAQ 2 and you'll practise the skill again later on. Turn back to SAQ 2 and refresh your memory of the typing chairs. Reread the answer to SAQ 2 and then answer SAQ 5.

SAQ 5

Write a title for this report.

'New Typing Chairs' (or something similar) would be a suitable title. The title of the report is important because it tells the reader directly, at first glance, exactly what it is you are discussing.

The introduction

Now that you have the title, and have checked its relevance, you can write the introduction to the report. An introduction can contain several different things, e.g.

- background to the topic
- aims of the report
- how the report is structured.

We suggest, though that you start by making your terms of reference clear, as this helps you to keep to the point.

Read the following example:

> ### NEW TYPING CHAIRS
>
> INTRODUCTION
>
> The purpose of this report is to advise the Office Manager on the most suitable chairs available for the typists. I examined three chairs and will discuss each of these in turn.

21

Notice:

- the relevant title
- the introduction which clearly states the purpose of the report and the reader for whom it has been prepared

SAQ 6

Go back to the Thorn 450K example, discussed in SAQ 1 and SAQ 3.

(a) Write down in your own words what the purpose of the report is
(b) Give the report a title
(c) Write an introduction which makes the purpose of the report clear

---

(a) . . . to investigate and report on why threads break in this machine (Thorn 450K).
(b) THREAD BREAKING IN THE THORN 450K
(c) INTRODUCTION

The purpose of this report is to examine and describe how and why threads keep breaking in the Thorn 450K.

There are two further things you will need to include in the introduction — any limitations on what you were able to do, and the method you used.

Limitations

You will always have to place limits on what you do — no-one has a lifetime to spend on one report and your reader will often want your report quickly. You will need to point out what, within the time, you were and were not able to do. Returning to the Thorn 450K, for example, you may need to say:

> I am awaiting precise information about the quality of threads used since this machine uses a different type of thread from our other machines.

SAQ 7———————————————————————

Look back to the report on the new typing chairs (SAQs 2 and 5). Write a sentence to indicate a limitation which the secretary writing that report may need to include.

———————————————————————

She may find only a very limited range of chairs available at that particular time and thus have to write 'Unfortunately only two models of chair were available in supplies'. (You may well have thought of other limitations.)

Method
Look back to the introduction to the report on the typing chairs (at the start of the section headed 'The introduction').

SAQ 8———————————————————————

Write out the sentence in the introduction which includes a reference to the method the writer has used.

———————————————————————

'I examined three chairs and will discuss each of these in turn.' This indicates clearly the method the writer has chosen to research into the topic and to meet the terms of reference. It also explains to the reader the way the writer has organised her report; this will help the Office Manager to find his way through it.

23

Conclusion

We have emphasised the importance of the terms of reference. These must *never* be forgotten. We have suggested a sequence that you can follow to get started:

- restate the terms of reference in your own words
- write a title
- write an introduction which shows that you are aware of the terms of reference and which includes a statement of
  - the method you used
  - any limitations you had to work under
  - how you have organised your report

We go on in the next chapter to look at how you can collect information for a report.

CHECK YOUR LEARNING

1. What element is missing from the following terms of reference?

> You have been attending a course at a college of further education. Prepare a report of what you have been doing and of your progress and submit it.

2. In the following example state (a) the reader of the report (b) (in your own words) its purpose (c) the person who has to *prepare* the report (d) the subject matter of the report.

> To a Works Foreman: 'We seem to be experiencing problems because of poor communication between the Machine Shop and the Chief Engineer. Please look into this and submit a report to the Plant Manager.'

3. We return to the case of the student attending a college of further education who has to prepare a report of her progress at college for one of her company's training officers. Read the following opening to a report to meet these terms of reference:

> ### REPORT ON MY ACTIVITIES AND PROGRESS AT COLLEGE
>
> #### INTRODUCTION
>
> So far I have found my time at college both stimulating and enjoyable. It is a purpose-built institution situated in pleasant countryside and was opened by Harold MacMillan in 1965. The college caters for a wide range of courses and also runs many interesting non-vocational courses.
>
> #### SPORTS FACILITIES
>
> The college has excellent sports facilities, an olympic-standard swimming pool, very experienced coaches and it offers awards for prowess in life-saving. Every student has to take some element of athletics in his or her course and it is safe to say that most students avail themselves of this wonderful opportunity.
>
> #### DRAMA CLUB
>
> And so on . . .

Do you think that this opening meets the terms of reference? Give reasons for your answer.

4. The Manager tells his Training Officer:

> 'We have to devise a training programme for the clerical staff and also for the storemen. Find out what you can and report back with some definite proposals.'

Read these terms of reference carefully. If you were the Training Officer, would you want to ask the Manager any further questions?

5.

> *To: The Deputy Manager*
> Please draw up a report listing the type of and number of complaints made by our customers last year (1983); be painstaking about this and look into every area — room service, restaurant, porter, menus, desk service, prices and so on. Suggest solutions to any problems you uncover.
>
> *Manager*

Imagine you are the Deputy Manager.

(a) Write down, in your own words, what the terms of reference require you to do.
(b) Give your report a title.
(c) Write an introduction which makes the purpose of the report clear.

6. Look back to question 1 — the student who has to prepare a report of her progress at a college of further education. Assume that you are the student but that your marks for the first term's exams are still not available and you have to use class assessment. How would you include this in the introduction?

7. Read the answer to question 5 — the introduction to the hotel report. There are four sentences in this introduction. Which sentence gives information about the *methods* the Deputy Manager has used?

8. An accountant is giving an interim report of the finances of a company. He states in his introduction that it is just a week before the month's trading figures are due. Why does he do this?

Answers to Check Your Learning
1. The *reader* is missing. Who is the report for? (In fact it is for a training officer, in this case.)

2. (a) The Plant Manager
(b) To improve communication between Machine Shop and Chief Engineer
(c) A works foreman
(d) Poor communication
(Or similar answers.)

3. Not really. The title is sound enough and so is the first sentence. The real trouble begins with the second sentence. The information from there on is just not relevant to the purpose — which is to find out what the student has been doing and how she has been progressing. The reader (the training officer) would not want to know about the range of courses offered, the sports facilities or the drama club — unless the writer could show what these have to do with the progress she's making at college.

4. The terms of reference are not as clear as they might be. The Training Officer might want to ask:

(a) Do you want *two separate* training programmes?

(b) What exactly do you want me to find out? About the *staff's* view of what's needed? The management's view? Both views? Other views (e.g. those of an outside consultant)?

(c) Are there any limits (e.g. time, money) which my proposals should bear in mind?

5.

(a) The Manager has asked me to inquire into all complaints made by customers last year and to recommend possible solutions to any problems I find.

(b) CUSTOMER COMPLAINTS (1983)

(c)

INTRODUCTION

The purpose of this report is to prepare a full survey and examination of all complaints made in the hotel last year. I have taken evidence from the suggestions box, from residents in the hotel at present, from long-stay and permanent residents and also from the staff in all departments. Complaints are examined under five main headings:

     Room service
     Restaurant service
     Bar facilities
     Staff/resident relations
     Miscellaneous.

I go on to suggest what we can do about these complaints.

ROOM SERVICE

Notice in (c) the way the writer proceeds to explain how the material is to be organised. We shall look at this topic, the collection and organisation of the material, in later chapters.

Your answers need not, of course, be exactly the same as those given here, which are only specimens. You should, though, check each answer carefully against ours and make sure that you are on the right lines.

6. You may add something like the following to your introduction:

Unfortunately, at the time of writing this report, my formal examination marks were not available. I am, however, submitting my marks for class assessment.

---

7. The *second* sentence. (The first sentence restates the terms of reference and the third tells us how the results of the investigation will be organised.)

8. He is stating limitations that govern what he has to say. The report may need modification when the trading figures are finally known. The accountant is taking care to ensure that his readers (or listeners) are aware of this.

ASSIGNMENT B_____

When you have agreed your topic with your tutor write down answers to the following questions:

Part 1
Subject matter   What is the subject matter of the report?
Purpose   What is the purpose of the report?
Reader   Who will read the report?
    What does the reader already know about the topic?
    What does the reader need to know?
    What use will the reader make of the report?

Part 2
Write a title and draft introduction and check your work against the checklist on p.96. Send both parts of this question to your tutor, adding a note of any difficulties you may have experienced in trying to answer it.

Collecting information

> **After you have worked through this chapter you should be able to:**
>
> ● list possible sources of the information necessary to write a report ☐
>
> ● say why it is important to keep a note of these sources ☐
>
> ● use 'spray notes' as a way of
>
>   — recording what you already know
>
>   — noting questions which you hope your sources will answer ☐
>
> ● use two methods of collecting information — A4 sheets of paper and 6″ × 8″ cards ☐

Sources of information

Most reports require you to collect information. This you can get from a variety of places.

SAQ 1_____

Look back at the examples given in the last unit — the Thorn 450K, the typing chairs, the college of further education, the hotel. (a) What kinds of information were used in each case? (You will find one or two under each.) (b) Add any further kinds you can think of which the report writer might have consulted, in each column. Some examples have been given to start you off.

Thorn 450K	Chairs	College	Hotel
	Supplies		Suggestions box

Thorn 450K	Chairs	College	Hotel	
Information about threads	Supplies Three chairs	Class assessments	Suggestions box Various resident staff	given in text
Interviewing operators Technical literature Manufacturer Other firms using the machine Suppliers	Brochures Other offices Technical reports	Exam results Comments on assignments Student's own view	Questionnaire to past residents Hotel neighbours	you may have thought of some of these - or others of your own

Some of this information will come direct from people (by letter, memo, telephone or simply through conversation); others from print (books, articles, etc.).

SAQ 2

Complete the following box, giving two examples of each from the above table.

Handwritten or typed	Word of mouth	Printed	May be any

Handwritten or typed	Word of mouth	Printed	May be any
Exam results	Interviewing operators	Technical literature	Manufacturer
Comment on assignments	Various residents	Brochures	Other firms
Suggestions box	Staff Supplies (people working there)	Technical reports	Suppliers
Questionnaire			Other offices Hotel neighbours

(You were only asked for two in each column.)

Some of your entries may be in different columns (e.g. in the hotel report the staff may be asked to fill in forms instead of being interviewed directly). The main point of the exercise is not for us to agree exactly which entry should go where but for you to see that it is possible to consult a whole variety of sources of information.

SAQ 3

Look at the answer to SAQ 1, first entry under Thorn 450K, 'Information about threads'. Would this 'information' be in the form of print, handwriting, typewriting or would it come from word of mouth (via a personal meeting or the telephone)?

Well, it could come in any of these forms. The information may be in a letter, contained in a phone call (e.g. from a supplier of thread) or in a printed technical report. Information may also be gained from an object itself, such as the three typist's chairs. By sitting in these chairs the report writer could find out a great deal about their comfort and convenience.

It is important to keep a note of where you get your information from. You may need to compare what one person says with another; or to check the claims made by one manufacturer with those made by another. You may need to return to one of your sources of information to find out more, later in your investigation. If you have no note of the source then you may waste a lot of time searching. Also, as we shall see later, it is necessary in some reports to write a list of your sources of information. Your reader may want to know where your ideas come from, so he can make allowances (he may think more highly of some sources than of others). You need only note very briefly where your information comes from (e.g. storekeeper; Agfa catalogue, *Which?* report; W. H. Smith).

We look next at ways in which you may collect information.

Spray notes

Before you actually turn to your sources of information it is a good idea to do two things — to write down what you already know about the subject of the report and to write down questions that you hope your sources will answer.

The notes you take at this stage will help to direct your later collection of information. You may, of course, prefer your own method of note-taking. As with all the advice given in this course, you are at liberty to set it to one side if you find that your own alternative way works better.

'Spray' notes (also called 'scatter', 'spider' or 'patterned' notes) are one way of recording your existing knowledge or any questions you want to ask. You write the subject at the centre of the page and write points off the sides. Let's say, for example, that you want to buy a bike. At the centre of a sheet of paper you write 'choice of bike'. Then you put down all relevant points around the sides, as below:

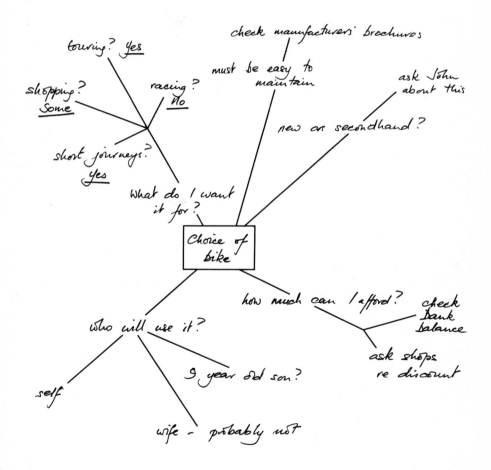

The spray notes have suggested both questions and possible sources of answers — and this whole process need take only a few minutes.

Complete the following box. (The first one is done for you.)

Question	Source(s) for answer
Ease of maintenance	Brochure

Question	Source(s) for answer
Ease of maintenance	Brochure
John What can I afford?	New or second hand? (1) bank balance (2) shops
Who will use it?	? discuss with wife and son

ACTIVITY

(For students working through this course without a tutor.) For the report you are writing use 'spray notes' in the way suggested above. Include in these notes some sources which you might consult to find out answers to your questions.

Collecting information

We have suggested spray notes as a useful way of beginning your search for information. How do you record this information once you actually start collecting it from your sources? There are several ways of doing this but we want to concentrate on two in the rest of this chapter — writing it onto A4 sheets and writing it onto cards (about 6″ × 8″). The A4 sheets method is very straightforward: as you find something you write it down (as briefly as possible, to save time) on the A4 sheet (A4 is the size of paper that fits comfortably into ring binders). Don't forget to add details of the source, for the reasons we gave earlier. Leave a gap beneath it, and *don't write on the back*, for reasons which will be clear when we come to the next chapter.

Not so many people are used to the cards method, so we'll discuss that more fully. You can buy small lined cards from stationery shops such as W. H. Smith and Menzies either 3″ × 5″ or 6″ × 8″ (we suggest the larger size) together with boxes for them to go into. But you don't even need to go to this expense: an elastic band or a bulldog clip will do instead of a box and you can use paper instead of card. You can, for example simply fold a sheet of A4 paper and tear it; do this twice and you get four sheets of paper of about the right size (keep all the paper the same size for convenience). It doesn't matter if this paper is used on one side since you need only one side blank.

Once you've got your paper (or, if you've got the money, the cards) you write each piece of information you collect onto a separate small sheet (or card) together with its source. You'll see in the next unit the value of this method. We show the two methods below.

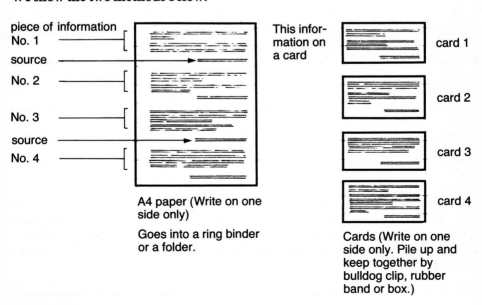

piece of information
No. 1
source
No. 2
No. 3
source
No. 4

A4 paper (Write on one side only)

Goes into a ring binder or a folder.

This infor-
mation on
a card

card 1

card 2

card 3

card 4

Cards (Write on one side only. Pile up and keep together by bulldog clip, rubber band or box.)

Try out one or both of these ways of collecting information in the reports which you have to write.

Conclusion

In this chapter we have shown the wide range of sources of information which you can consult when preparing a report. We have also suggested the value of spray notes at the early stages of planning your collection of information, and of A4 paper and cards when you are actually writing down answers to the questions you have posed.

CHECK YOUR LEARNING

1. In the previous chapter we gave terms of reference for a report as follows:

   To a Works Foreman . . . 'We seem to be experiencing problems because of poor communication between the Machine Shop and the Chief Engineer. Please look into this and submit a report to the Plant Manager.'

   Would you say that the information for this report would be gained

   (a) mainly through personal contact and discussions
   (b) though reading printed material
   (c) from objects in the factory?

2. Which of the following are sound reasons for keeping a note of the various sources of your information?

   (a) to prepare a list of sources to add to the end of your report
   (b) to make your report seem impressive
   (c) to return to a source later to find out more
   (d) to avoid giving your own view
   (e) to make it easier to compare what one source says with what another says

3. Your workmates have asked you to organise a party. Use the 'spray notes' technique suggested in the chapter to write down (a) questions you will need to answer and (b) possible sources of answers to these questions. Don't forget to write the topic (PARTY) in the centre of the page.

Answers to Check Your Learning
1. (a) The Foreman would not learn anything about poor communication in his place of work either from objects in the factory or from reading reports or books. He would have to go and *talk* to the people concerned. (He may just possibly also use a questionnaire.)

2. (a), (c) and (e) are sound reasons. (b) is unwise — your reader will almost certainly see through this tactic. (d) is wrong: the views of others are no substitute for your own — you are asked to report because your reader expects you personally to organise and comment on the views of others.

3.

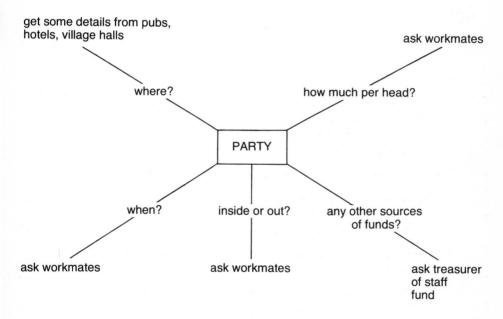

You will probably have something very different. Just check that you too have (a) questions (b) sources for answers.

Organising the information

After you have worked through this chapter you should be able to:
- **organise points in a logical order** ☐
- **plan your report** ☐
- **link the various sections together** ☐

First, let's return to the case of Karen Smith, the student at the college of further education. She has to write a report on what she has been doing and on her progress. Let's say that she has produced the following report. Read it through carefully. There are some questions on it below.

INTRODUCTION

The purpose of this report is to let my employers know how I am getting on in my day-release course at Blankshire College of Further Education.

I enjoy the college very much as I have made many friends there and I also find the subjects very interesting. English is perhaps my most difficult subject, but I also find Office Practice not so easy. In English we have to learn to write business letters, reports, memoranda but we sometimes get things like this in Office Practice. I like Shorthand and Typing and I believe that I am making progress in my speed, especially at Typing where I can now do 40 words a minute. Office Practice is a very useful subject. You learn to set up and operate a filing system and to use the many machines that you would expect to find in an office. The most modern machines are plain paper copiers which can produce about five copies a second. The English teachers are often very understanding and give us interesting books to read and we also get a good deal of vocabulary work and reference work. Unfortunately, my English marks were not available last week but I was given 58 for my English continuous assessment. I also got 70 for Office Practice since I am good at typing stencils and I enjoy working the duplicator. We also get some library work to do and we have two periods a week in the gym. I hope to get my Shorthand speeds up in the next few months and my teacher told me that I was starting to make good progress in the subject — Shorthand is mostly memory work. I find that I am making progress too in English comprehension and in summary. I quite like doing memos and minutes and agendas but we also do this in Office Practice.

All in all I feel that I am making good progress in my course. In project work and continuous assessment I have passed all subjects but my formal exam marks have not yet come from the examiners and I'll let you know when they arrive.

SAQ 1

If you were the Training Officer reading this report could you have a clear view of the student's progress? Does the student present the information clearly? Read the report again and give your views. Make a list of brief points in answer to this SAQ before you read on.

The Training Officer would have quite a job to sort out all the information. Karen has jumbled everything up and has left her reader to rearrange it. This is a very common fault in report writing. Your list might have included some of the following points:

- No subject headings in the body of the report
- Poor classification
- Conclusions occur at random
- Bad balance, e.g. shorthand and typing — two main elements — are barely mentioned
- No statement of how the report may be affected because of the absence of her exam results
- She gives continuous assessment marks only and it's not made clear what these mean (presumably they must be percentages).

The main problem lies in the way Karen has organised the material — or rather in the fact that she hasn't really organised the material at all. One way of avoiding this common problem is to decide on headings into which the material can be sorted to make a plan. Here, for example, is a plan for a report on how to use a new piece of equipment:

40

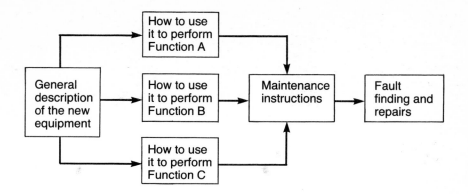

(From *'100% Report Writing: a guide for graduates and students'* by R. A. Ward, Thames Polytechnic)

You will notice that this plan gives not only section headings but also shows their relationship to one another.

Look again at Karen Smith's report. One fairly straightforward way of planning this would be to group the information under the subjects studied.

SAQ 2

If we chose 'subjects studied' as a way of classifying the information, what might the headings be?

English, Office Practice, Shorthand, PE and Typing. (You could also add a 'General' category for points which don't belong under any particular subject heading.)

SAQ 3

Go through the report and rearrange the material under these headings. One way of doing this is to use the box below. Summarise points in one or two words — don't copy out all the original words and phrases.

41

English	Office practice	Shorthand	PE	Typing	General

You should have something like what follows, though you will probably have used different words in places.

English	Office practice	Shorthand	PE	Typing	General
business letters reports memos minutes finds it difficult understanding teachers books to read vocabulary work reference work marks unavailable continuous assessment	business letters memos minutes finds it difficult finds it useful set up filing system use machines copier (5 copies per second) typing stencils duplicator	likes it progress in speed memory work	2 periods a week	likes it progress in speed (40 wpm)	enjoys it friends passed all subjects formal exam results yet to come

library work					
English compre-hension summary					

We shall return to Karen Smith's report later.

When writing the main body of a report (the part following the introduction and coming before the conclusion) it is important to sequence the headings in an order that makes sense. The next example gets you to do this.

The committee running the Fernhill Adventure Playground has been asked to write a report on the project for a committee in a neighbouring town which itself hopes to set up such a playground. Four paragraphs of this report follow, but *they have been deliberately placed out of order.*

SAQ 7—————————————————————————————————

What order would you place the paragraphs in? They have been numbered for easy reference, so your answer need be simply four numbers in a particular order.

1. THE PLAYGROUND
   The playground is well laid out with swings, trestles, scaffolding and cycle courses. Material is provided to let the children make 'dens' and in the summer time they can have tents and they are encouraged to erect the tents themselves. Mothers can accompany the children and there are rooms for painting and drawing. The playground opens at 9 a.m. and closes at 7 p.m. in both summer and winter.

2. BACKGROUND
   The playground was set up in 1974 after some of the stalwarts on the local community council had visited similar ventures in Liverpool and Manchester. The money was provided partly by the town council, partly through fund-raising and partly from a grant from the European Economic Community's Social Fund.

3. THE DISTRICT OF FERNHILL
   Fernhill is a working class area with a mixed population (about one quarter is Asian). It is classified as an area of multiple deprivation and large parts of the

neighbourhood have been pulled down leaving unsightly half-demolished tenements, crumbling walls, naked sites. Most of the shops have gone, leaving only a few public houses and betting shops.

4. THE FUTURE
The committee hope to develop a Community Education Centre and to obtain more premises in the form of portable huts. It would then be possible to run classes in literacy, basic numeracy, social and life skills. Negotiations with interested bodies are presently taking place.

Do not read on until you have written down your own suggested sequence.

You may have one of two sequences: 2, 3, 1, 4 *or* 3, 2, 1, 4. There's not much doubt that (4) should go last — it refers to what is *yet* to happen. What about the opening? You may choose to open with reference to the background to the playground, i.e. (2), or the area itself (3). Both (2) and (3) are 'background' paragraphs and so they should come before the description of the playground itself (1).

A4 sheets and cards
In the previous chapter you practised collecting information on either A4 sheets or cards. Once you have collected the information, you need to organise it and this is what you have been practising in this chapter. How can you resequence information recorded in these two ways?

A4 sheets
We mentioned in the last unit that you should

- use only one side of the paper
- leave a space after each item of information.

You can put the information into the order that suits you by using the following simple technique.

1. Cut up the sections into slips of paper

cut out each item

2. Put these into the sequence in which they will appear in the finished report. If you wish, you can stick the slips back onto A4 sheets in the new order.

Cards
These can simply be shuffled and reshuffled until the points are in the best order. Then you can write them up into paragraphs.

Signposts
Whichever method you choose you should make sure that you attend to the links between sections. Your reader will need signposts to see how the report is structured, how one section links to those before and after it. He is on a journey through your report and, like any other traveller, needs to see where he is going.

So, particularly in longer reports, your sections will need to begin and end with sentences such as 'I have given the five reasons for a change. But what *kind* of change is necessary? In the next section I discuss the alternatives.' You can insert such linking sentences into your plan — whether on A4 sheets or on cards.

In this chapter we have emphasized the importance of

- sorting material into logical sections
- putting these sections into a logical order
- attending to links between sections.

Longer reports will make greater demands in all these respects (e.g. longer sub-sections, the need to connect paragraphs together) but your work in this chapter should at least have laid the foundation for more advanced report writing.

The Check Your Learning section gives you a further opportunity to practise the very important skills introduced in this chapter. It's a long exercise this time but one that we strongly suggest you should try.

CHECK YOUR LEARNING

For this extended exercise we return to the hotel example used in Check Your Learning for Chapter 2 (question 5). Look back at that question to refresh your memory of

- the terms of reference
- the title
- the introduction.

You will remember that the Deputy Manager in his introduction says that he has collected evidence from a variety of sources and has organised this under five headings.

1. What are these headings?

2. The Deputy Manager in fact collected the following complaints, numbered for ease of reference:

   (1) Dirty linen on bed
   (2) Bar — interminable wait for service
   (3) Lights not working
   (4) Desk clerks chatting whilst there was a queue for service
   (5) Limited menu available
   (6) No flowers in room
       Long wait for room service breakfast to appear
   (7) Very small measure. One sixth of a gill at £1 a glass — ridiculous prices

(8) Crockery not properly washed (34 complaints)
(9) Garage closed much too early
(10) Internal phones not working
(11) Porter put letter in wrong pigeon-hole
(12) Waitress not very clean (12 complaints)
(13) Sheets not changed regularly
(14) Showers in rooms 14, 19, 21, 27 not working
(15) Bill not properly made up. Clerk was careless and insolent
(16) Bed and breakfast fee far too high
(17) Dinner not properly cooked. Ordered steak rare done —
   convinced it was braised steak
(18) Table not properly laid — no fish knives
(19) Wine served as 'lambrusco' — was definitely *not* lambrusco
(20) TV in Room 44 not working — customer was promised
   replacement but nothing done
(21) 'Piped' music in bar very loud
(22) Non-residents using residents' Lounge Bar
(23) Porter made no effort to help elderly customer with a heavy
   case to lift
(24) Loud and angry voices from the kitchen — very off-putting
(25) Room decoration

Sort these out into the five headings given above. (Use a box like this if you wish.) Do not write out each point in full; just write down the number.

- Staff/resident relations
- Miscellaneous

2.

Room service	Restaurant service	Bar facilities	Staff/ resident relations	Miscel- laneous
1	5	2	4	3
6	8	7	11	9
10	12	21	15	
13	17	22	23	16
14	18			
20	19			
25	24			

ASSIGNMENT C

Part 1 Use spray notes (or another method of your own) to record
- what you already know about the topic of your report
- what you need to know (your questions)
- where you might find this information.

(Make sure your handwriting is clear enough for your tutor to read.)

Part 2 Collect the information

Part 3 Organise the information into groups, with headings for each group (or 'section').

Check your work by referring to the checklists on pp. 96-8. Then send the results of your work on 1 and 3 to your tutor.

CHAPTER FIVE

Writing conclusions and recommendations

After you have worked through this chapter you should be able to:

● **write an effective conclusion** ☐

● **write clear recommendations** ☐

● **see how conclusions and recommendations relate to terms of reference, title and introduction** ☐

The conclusion

We said in Chapter One that reports are written for busy people to help them to take a decision. They will turn quickly to the end of a report to see what the writer recommends. If they cannot *find* the conclusion, or if the conclusion is vague, then they will be disappointed. So the conclusion to a report is very important. It should

* refer back to the *purpose* of the report
* state main points arising from the report
* be conclusive
* be brief.

SAQ 1_____

Look back over your work in Chapter 4. Pull out possible main points from Karen Smith's report for use in a conclusion. Use the box below if you wish.

Subject	Main point(s)

Office Practice	
English	
Typing	
Shorthand	

Subject	Main point(s)
Office practice	reasonable; parts are difficult
English	could improve ...
Typing	some progress, but still slow
Shorthand	some progress

You may have different material from ours but the main thing is that you shouldn't have tried to include too much. Remember — a conclusion needs to be brief and it should refer back to the *main purpose* of the report. In this case, the main purpose is really to get an idea from Karen of how well she is getting on, of what progress she is making. Particularly important for this reader (the Training Officer) would be any marks and grades, and these are what we have concentrated on.

SAQ 2

Using your work (and ours) in SAQ 1, write a conclusion to the report on Karen Smith. Imagine that you are Karen Smith (i.e. use 'I').

> I could improve my English work; my report writing in particular needs attention. My typing is also disappointing: 40 words per minute is slower than I should be achieving. My continuous assessment marks in English, Office Practice and Shorthand are quite good but I must wait for the marks from the exams before I can feel confident about saying this.

This, or something like it, would meet the characteristics of a good conclusion, as outlined earlier in this chapter. (You may well have decided to highlight different points from your list in Chapter 4.)

Now try the next example, which starts with a memo sent from a Housing Sub-Committee to the Council's Properties Section.

> To: PROPERTIES SECTION
> The Housing Sub-Committee of Newtown Town Council at its meeting on Monday 24th October 1983 decided to explore the possibility of buying a property at 110 Stock Street. The hope is that it will be possible to adapt the house for use as a Day Care Centre for elderly people. Please view the house and report on its suitability. This is urgent; but bear in mind that funds are limited — we cannot exceed £20,000.

The surveyor reported as follows:

> INTRODUCTION
> The purpose of this report is to give the Housing Sub-Committee an outline of the suitability of the property at 110 Stock Street for conversion to a Day Centre for the elderly. I have made the report as extensive as possible, bearing in mind the urgency imposed by the terms of reference and the fact that others are interested in the property.
>
> HOUSE AT 110 STOCK STREET
> This is a solid greystone dwelling of two storeys, with eight rooms, a kitchen and two bathrooms, one upstairs and one downstairs. The house is about 60 years old and is in basically good condition. The bathrooms are large and could be adapted for elderly and infirm people quite easily. There is some dampness at the back of the house but this is probably because the house has been empty for some time.
>
> ACCOMMODATION
> The rooms are of varied sizes; four are large, 6m × 8m, and the others are about 5m × 4m. They could accommodate a variety of activities: lectures, games, film shows, handicrafts. The kitchen is large and square and adjoins a large room which could easily be adapted to become a dining room.

TRANSPORT

The house is close to bus and train stations and it also has ample car-parking facilities to the rear.

PRICE

£18,000 or offers near to that. The rateable value is £600 per annum. The Council, with an *early* bid, should succeed in buying the house for £18,000.

THE AREA

The street (Stock Street) is rather busy with traffic and shoppers and there is a betting shop about 100 yards away on the other side. There is a public house about 200 yards away and the betting shop does tend to attract undesirable elements. This need not matter, though, as the hours of the Day Centre are likely to mean that residents would be little disturbed.

CONCLUSION

The house seems a good buy but there are undesirable factors in the area.

P. Kirby
Properties Section
Newtown Town Council

SAQ 3

Check back to the points made earlier in this chapter about a good conclusion. Is this conclusion

- *brief*
- *conclusive?*

Does it

- *state the main points arising from the report*
- *refer back to the purpose of the report?*

The conclusion is brief — too brief and it falls down on the other points. It is inconclusive and the main findings of the report are not re-stated. The report seems to be moving towards the conclusion 'buy the house'. If you check back through you'll see that nearly everything that is said about the house itself is favourable. The house is soundly built, in good condition, with suitable sized rooms, could be easily converted. It is well placed for transport and it could almost certainly be bought for a good bit less than the Council is prepared to spend. The only two problems mentioned — some dampness and the area — are not (in the main body of the report) considered to be too serious. The conclusion starts decisively but ends feebly, with the comment on the area itself. The surveyor doesn't seem to have gone far enough: other buyers are waiting and the Council should act quickly. He should have said this more clearly.

SAQ 4

Write your own conclusion to the above report, bearing these points in mind and adding any further details of your own.

CONCLUSION

The house seems a good buy. It could be adapted easily for use as a Day Centre, and at low cost. The area itself has some problems but these need not worry the elderly people: the public house should be quiet during the day and the betting shop is a good distance away. The house is of solid stone and this (with the addition of double glazing) will insulate the senior citizens from traffic noise. Since other buyers are interested our recommendation is for the Council to put in a bid of £18,000 as quickly as possible.

We think that this meets the conditions for an effective conclusion. Check your own conclusion to see if you are happy with it or whether you want to modify it.

SAQ 5

Turn to the work you carried out in Check Your Learning for Chapter Four on the hotel example. Write an effective conclusion to that report. We suggest that you use the steps recommended in SAQ 1, i.e. pick out main points from each section (Room Service, etc.) and then write these main points up into a conclusion. To make sure you are brief we suggest that you write no more than one sentence for each of the sections.

In the suggested answer notice the way the writer returns to the purpose of his report, in the first sentence. There follow four sentences summarising the main problems. The last sentence leads the reader on into a further section. (The Deputy Manager has decided to leave out the 'Miscellaneous' complaints, probably because there is little that can be done about them.)

Recommendations

We've just remarked that the last line of the suggested conclusion mentions another section. You may have thought that a conclusion is a conclusion and nothing need follow. But in some reports, and particularly in longer ones, it is clearer to have a separate section stating any recommendations the writer wishes to make. These may include suggested actions (and who should take them) and any further investigations necessary.

SAQ 6

Put yourself in the place of the Deputy Manager. Write a set of recommendations for the Manager's consideration.

RECOMMENDATIONS
Room Service
- Bed linen should be changed every morning in every room whether the resident is long or short stay
- The third floor must be redecorated this winter
- Maids and porters must be reminded of the importance of speedy and courteous room service

Recommendations should be clearly laid out and they should arise logically from the conclusion.

You have now practised writing all major parts of a report:

- Title
- Introduction
- Main body
- Conclusion
- Recommendations.

We have also stressed (in Chapter Two and throughout) the importance of the terms of reference. In a good report all these things are closely connected:

Title	should be relevant	
	restates terms of reference	
Introduction	states method used	
	refers to any limitations	
	gives plan	
Main body	material is grouped to deal with main aspects of the topic as mentioned in the introduction	All are planned to meet the terms of reference — i.e. the purpose of the report,
Conclusion	collects *main* points and	and its reader

55

	restates them conclusively. refers back to terms of reference
Recommendations	state any proposed action necessary
	(In shorter reports, recommendations can be put into the conclusion.)

In a good report the reader can look at the title and then the conclusion and should see that the one follows from the other. Similarly the conclusion and the introduction should fit together.

Now that we have considered all the main parts of a report we can move on to look at questions of style and presentation.

ACTIVITY

Consult reports, available in your place of work, college or library. Read titles, introductions and conclusions and see if they hold together well. Look also at the main headings given in the main body of the report — do these seem relevant to the topic?

CHECK YOUR LEARNING

1. Which of the following applies to an effective conclusion?
     (a) it is brief
     (b) it includes new information
     (c) it always includes recommendations
     (d) it is conclusive

2. Say why, in one sentence, it is important to write an effective conclusion to a report.

3. Write a sentence saying what should go into a section headed 'Recommendations'.

4. In the Check Your Learning for Chapter Two we quoted the case of a Works Foreman asked to meet the following terms of reference —

> We seem to be experiencing problems because of poor communication between the Machine Shop and the Chief Engineer. Please look into this.

(a) Do you think that such a report would have a section headed 'Recommendations'? Give a brief reason for your answer.

(b) If so, write one recommendation the Foreman could possibly make. (You'll need to use your imagination here.)

Answers to Check Your Learning

1. (a) and (d). (b) is wrong; conclusions should not include new information — they re-state the most important points that have already been made in the report. (c) is wrong because of the word 'always'; conclusions sometimes do include recommendations but on other occasions there may be a separate section headed 'Recommendations'.

2. Something like:

> The reader (probably busy) will want to see at a glance which points the writer considers important.

3. Something like:

> In this section the writer gives his/her own views on what action needs to be taken in the light of the report.

4. (a) There is no absolute right or wrong answer to this one. The terms of reference are vague; what does 'look into' mean exactly? Does it

include making recommendations or just explaining why poor communication has occurred? Also, you may have said that the report would be short and that any recommendations would be included in the conclusion.

Or you may have said 'Yes. The Plant Manager would expect some recommendations and would be looking for them to be clearly stated.' This kind of answer would also be acceptable. What is important is that, whatever your answer, you gave a reason for it.

(b) This is an artificial exercise since we cannot know what the Foreman would find. But using our imagination we can suggest recommendations like the following:

There should be a weekly meeting between the Manager, the Machine Shop and the Chief Engineer with a note taken of any decisions made.

The Machine Shop should be asked to take more notice of memos.

The Chief Engineer should appoint a representative to liaise with the Machine Shop.

(You were asked for one recommendation only and you may well have thought of other possibilities.)

Planning paragraphs

After you have worked through this chapter you should be able to:

- **say what makes a successful paragraph** ☐
- **write paragraphs that are clear, and complete in themselves** ☐

In the previous chapters we have practised the overall grouping of material into sections. But each section must then be written up into one or more paragraphs and it is here that people often meet difficulties. It's all too easy to shirk the task of writing clear paragraphs.

In this chapter we suggest some simple rules for writing well-planned paragraphs. You may notice that not all the paragraphs in this book conform to these rules. There are two reasons for this: first, this is an instructional text, *not* a report; and second, you are learning how to master the basics of writing. Experienced writers know when and how to break the rules — indeed, if you are one we suggest you omit this chapter altogether.

First, what *is* a paragraph? Generally a paragraph deals with one point fully. It states clearly what this point is, discusses it, and makes sense on its own. A paragraph should thus

- contain a sentence (often called a 'topic' sentence) which makes clear what the paragraph is about
- elaborate on the topic sentence
- include information related only to that one topic and no other.

Paragraphs are enormously useful: they help *you* to break the writing task into manageable chunks and they help *your reader* to take in your meaning.

SAQ 1_____

Read the following:

> There are three ways in which the river is of value to the community. First, it gives opportunities to the villagers to enjoy their leisure — fishing, boating, swimming. Next, it brings trade into the area: holidaymakers on canal barges visit local pubs and shops. And thirdly it is a trade route for local goods out to Harcourt.

- *underline the topic sentence*
- *say how each of the other sentences contributes to the main idea.*

The first sentence shows clearly what the rest of the paragraphs will be about; the reader is left in no doubt. The rest of the paragraph discusses the three ways in which the river is of value and gives examples. The structure of the paragraph could be shown like this:

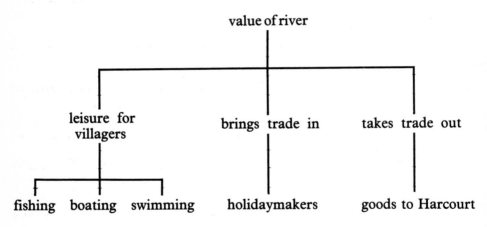

Such clearly organised, well planned paragraphs are easy for the reader to 'take in'.

Before you can write a clear paragraph you must obviously know what the main idea is that you want to communicate. But what often happens is that the writer is unclear as to the main idea and opens with a sentence that is vague or that tries to include too much. Like this, for example:

> The century has been one of change and it is possible to discern two strong areas into which the population may divided.

SAQ 2

What is wrong with this?

We can see two things wrong. Firstly, there are *two* mains ideas rather that one. Secondly, what does the second part of the sentence mean?

SAQ 3

What are the two main ideas?

1. This has been a century of change.
2. The population can be divided into two strong (main?) areas (groups? geographical areas?).

Running the two ideas together means that neither is clear. The writer cannot elaborate both ideas at once. Here is another example:

> I quite like doing minutes and memos. But we also do this in English.

Is the writer on the point of saying that she believes the repetition of the subjects in English made it less enjoyable? We can't be sure — she hasn't made her meaning clear.

Let's now return, for practice, to Karen Smith's report. You'll remember that we had sorted out the information into chunks (see p. 42). Our next job is to write each up clearly into separate paragraphs.

SAQ 4_____

Write up the section on Office Practice into one paragraph using some or all of the information given in the office-practice column. Write straightforward sentences. Don't forget to start with a clear topic sentence.

You should have something like this:

> Office Practice is a very varied subject. It has areas of overlap with Business English. You have to learn how to set up and operate a filing system in the office and to be able to use the many machines that you would expect to find in an office. We have plain-paper copiers which can produce about five copies every second, and we have to be able to type stencils and operate a duplicator.

All of the paragraph is concerned with Office Practice, though it is perhaps not as fluent as it might be. The topic sentence stresses how varied the subject is and some details from the column (e.g. its difficulty) are omitted. It is at this stage in report writing that you will usually find you can discard some of the information you have collected, for reasons of space or relevance, or to communicate more clearly with your reader.

SAQ 5_____

Practise further the important skill of writing clear paragraphs by writing up the section on English.

Here's our attempt:

> I can give a summary of my English work though unfortunately my formal results are not yet available. We write business letters, reports, memos and minutes and we undertake vocabulary and reference work. We prepare summaries and complete

comprehension exercises. Reading is also an important part of the course, including study in the library. I find the subject difficult but fortunately we have understanding teachers. My continuous assessment mark is 58%.

Notice the way the points have been presented in this paragraph. In particular there is a clear first sentence making the important point about the lack of exam results and letting the reader see what he can expect from the rest of the paragraph. Writing activities are grouped together, and then reading. The last but one sentence puts together two points which otherwise would be 'bitty'.

So in writing a paragraph try to

- start with a sentence which indicates what the paragraph is about
- group related points together, to avoid a string of unrelated bits and pieces.

CHECK YOUR LEARNING

We return to the Deputy Manager's report. In the Check Your Learning for Chapter Four we had sorted the points into logical groups. We know that the Deputy Manager has decided on an order for his report. (See Check Your Learning, Chapter Four.)

The next step is to write one or more paragraphs under each heading.

1. What should you try to do when writing paragraphs?
2. Write one paragraph on the first heading, Room Service. Carry out the advice on paragraph writing given above. You can slightly change the details if you wish: use the list of points made under Check Your Learning, question 2, Chapter Four, as a guide and, if you wish, fill out the information using your imagination.

The remainder of these questions are optional. We strongly recommend you to try them if you have any difficulty with writing paragraphs. Compare your own paragraphs carefully with ours.

3. Write a paragraph (or paragraphs) on the restaurant service.
4. Write a paragraph (or paragraphs) on the bar facilities, using the original list of complaints as a basis, as before.
5. Now conclude the exercise by writing paragraphs for each of the last two headings: Staff/resident relations and Miscellaneous.

Answers to Check Your Learning

1. You should have one or more of:
   - start with a sentence which sums up the content of the paragraph
   - group points together logically within the paragraph
   - contain information relevant to that topic and none other.

2. Here's one possible paragraph (yours will be different):

> There were a number of complaints about room service and my investigations have found these to be justified. (A full list of complaints is given as Appendix One.) Fortunately these are not all serious and many of the minor ones can easily be put right (e.g. dirty linen, lack of flowers in rooms, speed of service). Some do, though, require more major action: several guests complained about the poor decoration on the third floor and it is in fact ten years since this was last painted. We must deal quickly with the minor points and make plans to remedy the more serious deficiencies. Room service is a vital area; the hotel rooms are our customers' second homes and we must provide the highest possible standard of service.

Notice the following points:
   - The paragraph is not just a list of complaints. The Deputy Manager has put them into an appendix so the Manager can check them if he wishes but so they don't get in the way of the report itself. (We'll mention appendices again later.)
   - The Deputy Manager has given his own interpretation of the points. He has distinguished between major and minor problems, between problems that can be dealt with quickly and those that will take more time. He not only begins the paragraph effectively, he closes it well, too.
   - These things will help the Manager to see, quickly, what *kind* of complaints have been made and how the causes of complaint can be remedied.

3.

> THE RESTAURANT
> There were a number of complaints about the restaurant and we must try to reduce these. The restaurant offers a service to outsiders as well as to residents and a high standard of service may well encourage customers to use all the facilities of our hotel.
> There were more complaints in this area than in any other: complaints about the limited menu available, that the crockery was not properly washed, about untidy waitresses, badly cooked meat and careless table service. It was also claimed that certain wines were misrepresented. One customer said that he could hear angry voices coming from the kitchen and I have subsequently found this to be true.

4.

> **THE BAR**
>
> One would expect a lot of complaints about the bar since it is the busiest part of the hotel, but fortunately there are relatively few. There were some complaints about the small measure for spirits but the measure and prices are those adopted by the trade generally. Some residents complained about the fact that non-residents were using the Residents' Lounge and there was one complaint about the loudness of piped music.
>
> There is nothing here to get particularly worried about, but we should do something about non-residents drinking in the Residents' Lounge and about the loudness of the music.

5.

> **STAFF/RESIDENT RELATIONS**
>
> This is an area that we must exercise firm control over. There were several complaints about Reception, especially about desk clerks not acting efficiently while customers were queuing up. There does seem to be some slackness in this area generally. The only other complaint concerned a misplacing of post but I could not find out which porter was involved.
>
> **MISCELLANEOUS**
>
> Many of the complaints in this category are not problems that we can do a great deal about. We have no real control over the telephone system and lifts do break down. We already have a fully operational maintenance scheme and since we only hire spaces in the garage we cannot really control its opening hours.

If you have persevered with these exercises then you will have gained considerable practice in writing clear paragraphs — a rare skill.

CHAPTER SEVEN

Writing clearly

After you have worked through this chapter you should be able to:
- **check that your writing style is clear** ☐
- **check that you are using an appropriate tone** ☐

In this chapter we look at one other important ingredient of a good report: the way in which the points are actually made in the written style. If the style is unclear or awkward then all the work at earlier stages will be wasted. On the other hand, careful and thorough work at these earlier stages is the best guarantee of the style coming right. So if you have carried out the advice given in this book and practised

- writing titles and introductions
- collecting information and sorting it into logical groups
- thinking about the structure of the paragraphs

then you should be very well placed to write clearly.

SAQ 1

Why is it so important to write clearly?

You may think that this is too obvious a question. We ask it because we want, once again, to remind you of the *point* of all this. Did you in fact give an answer such as 'Because it's got to be read' or 'To help the reader get the message' or 'So the reader can see possible courses of action open to him'? We hope so.

Thinking of your reader

Bearing your reader in mind throughout helps you decide both what to say and how to say it. We said earlier that you should remember both what he knows (you need only to refer briefly to that) and what he doesn't but needs to know (you'll have to spell that out fully). Technical language is an example. Some key words (especially if they are from new technologies) may not be familiar to your reader, or he may use them in a different way from the way in which you want to use them. To make sure that you are both talking about the same thing, it helps to identify such words in advance and to define them — either when you first use them, or in the introduction, or in an appendix (in which case you would need to refer the reader from the text to the appendix). In this connection, you should be particularly careful never to use an abbreviation without first giving the word or title in full, e.g. Anglian Water Authority (AWA). Once you have done this you can then use the abbreviation for the remainder of the report.

Don't try to impress your reader by blinding him with science or by using complicated, technical language just for its own sake. Address him directly. Some reports may need an impersonal style but usually, in the real world, the use of 'I' or 'we' is perfectly permissible — and this is just as well since it can cut out a lot of unnecessary wordiness.

Tone

Thinking of your reader also helps you to use the correct tone — the most appropriate way of addressing your particular reader. It is best as a general rule to be direct and straightforward. Common faults are

- being too slapdash and trendy ('There is no way that will be done')
- being too pompous ('I would suggest . . . It is incumbent on us all to . . .')
- being aggressive and controversial.

SAQ 2_____

Imagine that the Deputy Manager of the hotel includes the following in his report:

It's clear that the desk staff are, not to put too fine a point on it, too lazy to lift a finger. Sack the lot, I say.

Is the tone suitable, do you think?

_____

This would be quite wrong in tone for the Deputy Manager's report — and for any other report, come to that. It is too aggressive, too much like speech rather than writing, and too full of the colloquial ('to lift a finger') and the clichéd ('not to put too fine a point on it'). Compare it with what the Deputy Manager actually wrote, in Chapter Five.

Another failing in tone is to ask rhetorical questions, i.e. statements in the form of questions to which only one answer is expected:

> It is surely to be expected that all engineers should know how to use a job sheet.

This expects only one answer — yes. A report should be in plain and unbiased language and the writer should not seek to influence the reader in any hidden way. (The sentence is also wordy — 'It is surely to be expected that . . .')

SAQ 3

Rewrite the sentence to free it of these problems.

> There is a good case for expecting all engineers to know how to use a job sheet.
>
> It is reasonable to assume that engineers know how to use a job sheet.

These alternatives say the same thing in a calmer, more objective way; there is no personal edge in the tone to upset the reader.

Accurate expression, or 'good English'

You need to check spelling and punctuation carefully since mistakes here can affect the meaning of what you write and the degree to which you succeed in communicating with your reader. We cannot, in this short book, go through the finer points of spelling and punctuation and these are not normally necessary anyway; as long as you get your meaning over the odd error is probably not significant. The booklist on pp. 100-101 suggests other books which you might buy and work through if spelling and punctuation are particular problems for you. In general, use only full stops and commas; this keeps your style simple.

ACTIVITY

Check the examples of reports we have given in this book. Would you call them well-written?

It's all too easy to write down *more or less* what you wanted to say, leaving the reader to carry out the final job of making it precise. But it is your job as writer to say exactly what you mean. The best way to write clear sentences is to

- think clearly about *exactly* what you want to say
- say one thing at a time
- imagine your reader(s) and ask: Will what I write communicate to them?

CHECK YOUR LEARNING

1. What do you think is wrong with the following:

   (a) The Deputy Manager in the report quoted earlier has a section explaining to the hotel Manager what job each employee carries out.

   (b) You are a surveyor reporting on a house which your client wishes to purchase. There is damp which is caused by poor plastering. If the client understands the matter fully then he can instruct the plasterer to use a certain mix. But it's a technicality and is hard to explain. So you don't elaborate.

2. The following are extracts from reports. What, if anything, is wrong with them:

   (a) It is proposed that the on-going situation is constantly reviewed.
   (b) At this point in time we can all see the merits of a clean sweep.

70

3. Put the following passage into plain English. (It may take a few minutes but this will be good practice.)

> All personnel, staff, manpower or workforce functioning or operating in the venue of the clerical department or divisional section must indicate to their supervisors that they have had the opportunity to take cognisance of this notice by an acknowledgement of receipt of same.

4. Rewrite in clear English the following conclusion to a report:

> It was found that by selection of the proper test conditions it was possible to duplicate the actual use of the machine by the housewife. Under these conditions, there was a definite tendency for the fan mechanism to deteriorate or to break down completely after usage which was equivalent to $3\frac{1}{2}$ years of service in the home. It is believed, therefore, that it is desirable to replace the fan mechanism by substituting the larger motor which is capable of 6 years of service under the same conditions.

(Taken from *Shurter et al.*, see booklist, Appendix Two)

5. Two ideas have been run together in the following opening sentence to a paragraph. Say what the two ideas are.

> The writer has dwelled on the suffering of the industrial population and their environment.

6.
> A not unanticipated consequence was that the building was unable to remain standing.

(a) What is wrong with this?
(b) Rewrite it.

7.

> It's pretty obvious, isn't it, that we should do something about
> people pinching things from the cloakroom.

(a) What is wrong with this?
(b) Rewrite it so that it could form part of a report.

Answers to Check Your Learning

1. (a) The writer has forgotten what his reader already knows — the
       Manager would not need to be told what job each employee carries out.
   (b) The writer should include this information; the reader needs to
       understand something of the causes of the damp so he can get the
       condition put right.
2. (a) This is wordy, impersonal and it contains worn-out phrases which
       sound grand but don't mean much ('on-going situation').
   (b) Again, worn-out wordy phrases — 'at this point in time . . . a clean
       sweep'.
3. It means something like:
       Every person in the section should let his/her supervisor know that
       they have seen this letter.
   The original is an example of an unnecessarily long and complicated
   sentence.
4. Something like:

> By selecting proper test conditions, we duplicated the housewife's actual use of
> the machine. These tests showed that the fan mechanism deteriorated or broke
> down after the equivalent of $3^1/_2$ years of service in the home. We believe the
> larger motor should be used because our tests show it can give 6 years of service
> under the same conditions.

Compare this closely with the original to see how much shorter and more
direct it is.

5. (a) the writer has dwelled on the suffering of the industrial population.
   (b) the writer has dwelled on the environment of the industrial
       population.
   You could argue that these are both parts of the same idea (i.e. what the

writer has dwelled on). Even so, the sentence is a dangerous one; could the writer clarify both sub-points in one paragraph?

6. (a) Too many negatives, and it's wordy.
   (b) As expected, the building fell down. *Or* The building fell down, as we expected. (Or something similar.)
7. (a) It's too colloquial ('pretty obvious'; 'pinching'). When writing reports you should be more formal (e.g. 'It is clear that . . .'; 'stealing'). Also, there's a rhetorical question expecting only one answer — 'It's pretty obvious, isn't it, that . . .' This is rather aggressive, not allowing the reader room to make up his own mind; the reader needs to be led towards conclusions, not bullied into them.
   (b) We should consider taking action to prevent thefts from the cloakroom. (Or something similar.)

ASSIGNMENT D

Part 1 Draft the conclusion and recommendations to your report, using as a guide the checklist on p. 97.

Part 2 Draft two or three paragraphs of the main body of your report, using the checklists on writing paragraphs and writing clearly on p. 97.

CHAPTER EIGHT

How to check your written work

After you have worked through this chapter you should be able to:
- **use a procedure for drafting and redrafting your work** ☐
- **check your report at all stages** ☐

This chapter sets out a way of writing reports which
- involves several drafts
- enables you to carry out a series of checks on your work.

The procedure is a simple one but means that you need to leave yourself time to carry out the final checks. Unfortunately, most people leave things too late and then have to dash off the report at the last minute.

First draft
Take your plan for the report (see Chapter Four) and move straight to a rough draft of the whole of it. At this stage concentrate just on getting down all you want to say; polishing comes later. Don't cram too many words onto each page because you'll certainly want to make some changes.

Then **check the structure** of what you have written:
- are the sections placed in a logical order?
- is the introduction clear?
- does your conclusion square with your terms of reference?

If you identify any problems then put these right by redrafting. (You may use 'scissors and paste' as suggested in Chapter Four, cutting out the weak section of your report and sticking a new one in.)

Then **check your expression**, using the advice given in the last chapter. You should be able to change words and phrases by crossing out and writing in new bits — hence the advice given above to leave space around your page. You may also need the scissors and paste again.

Then if possible **use another person**. If your work is legible enough this other person (a friend or colleague) can read your report and write his or her comments on it. Or (if the report is short) you can read it aloud to him/her asking him/her for comment on both structure and style — e.g. Does it flow? Is it in logical order? Is anything omitted? Is anything repeated too many times? The comments of another person are of enormous value. It can be difficult to take criticism but it's better for it to come from a friend rather that from the reader for whom the report is prepared. Make any further changes you feel are necessary, using those of your friends' criticisms that you feel are worth acting on.

Then **make your final draft** (Chapters Nine, Ten and Eleven and their checklists should be consulted here.)

'Proof-read' your final draft for any typing or other errors which may have crept in.

Sired by the Royal Stallion, the Queen could not but feel satisfaction at the result.
(London newspaper)

BEATLES John Lennon and Paul McCartney composed a song—under a pen name—to see how it would do in the charts without their reputation to push it.
Four weeks after the song was recorded, the disc is TWENTY-THIRD in the charts.
The song is Woman. The disc was made by Peter and Gordon. Paul's girl friend, Jane Asher, is Peter's brother.
Daily Mirror

Police said that about 40,000 people wee at the shine and the stampede occued when the cush of people on the twenty five-foot wide staiway ushed to get the taditional ice cakes thown by a piest, boke down a nine-foot guad wall and its stone and concete, mingled with sceaming, falling people, landed on the cowds below.—Reute.

What happens when proof-reading is neglected.

If you count up the stages listed above you'll see that there are six. This may put you off, but before you throw this book in the wastepaper basket remember one thing. *None of these stages need take very long*, particularly the last five. And they not only lead to better reports; they also make you more self-critical and likely to write a better report, more quickly, next time. These stages are, in fact, those adopted by anyone who writes seriously. Novelists, journalists and writers of textbooks will all vouch for the value of

- making a rough draft, not worrying too much about the accuracy of the language

- checking overall structure
- checking detailed expression
- trying the writing out on friends and listening to their criticisms
- drafting and redrafting until it's right
- checking the final manuscript for typing errors
- using scissors and paste techniques.

ACTIVITY 1

If you have any friends or colleagues who write regularly, ask them how they set about the job of writing. Ask them what they think of the advice given in this book.

ACTIVITY 2

Try this sequence out when writing your reports. Or just try out one or two parts of it and see what difference this makes.

CHECK YOUR LEARNING

1. Put the following suggested stages into the right order.
   - check for language, and change as necessary
   - proof-read
   - make your rough draft
   - check for structure and change as necessary
   - use another person's comments and change report as necessary

2. Give *two* (or more) reasons for carrying out these stages.

Answers to Check Your Learning

1. make your rough draft
   check for structure and change as necessary
   check for language and change as necessary
   use another person's comments and change report as necessary
   make your final draft
   proof-read

2. • none of the stages need take you very long
   • by following the stages you will produce a better report
   • you will become more self-critical
   • you will write better reports more quickly in future
   • this is the way professional writers operate.
   (You may have thought of other reasons of your own.)

Layout

After you have worked through this chapter you should be able to:
- use a checklist to ensure that your report is properly laid out ☐

In Chapter One we identified four features in the report format.

SAQ 1_____

What were these four features?

_____

      Title
      Introduction
      Main body (with sub-headings)
      Conclusion

In Chapter Five we added one other possible feature — recommendations. We wanted as far as possible to discuss just the key features. But reports vary greatly in their length and scope, as you'll see if you go and look at the collections of government and other reports in your local library. You may be required to submit reports with sections which we have not yet mentioned. In this chapter we begin by considering some further features.

ACTIVITY 1_____

Are you aware of any special features which should be included in your reports?

If you are unsure, ask your supervisor, teacher or training officer. Or consult a colleague. You may be expected to produce a **title page**. This would be not more than the title of the report together with the name of the person (or committee) responsible for producing the report. The **date** of the report should always be given; some reports quickly become dated and *future* readers will need to know when the report was originally written. On the title page, or on a separate sheet, you may be asked to include a **table of contents**. This simply lists the main sections of your report together with the page numbers.

SAQ 2

Draw up a contents page for the hotel example. Use the relevant parts of earlier chapters to help you do this. (You need not in this case insert page numbers.)

INTRODUCTION .... p.

ROOM SERVICE .... p.

RESTAURANT SERVICE .... p.

BAR FACILITIES .... p.

STAFF/RESIDENT RELATIONS p.

MISCELLANEOUS .... p.

CONCLUSION .... p.

RECOMMENDATIONS .... p.

You may wish to **number** the various sections of your report. There are several ways of doing this — letters (e.g. A, B, C) or numbers (1, 2, 3). You may need a combination of these. You may (especially in a longer report) want to break a section up into shorter sections and to make it clear exactly where each of these sub-sections belongs. Let's return to SAQ 2 to show this. The Deputy Manager may wish to indicate that items 2-6 inclusive on the list are all parts of a larger whole — the 'analysis of the complaints' (or something similar). In that case he would put ANALYSIS OF COMPLAINTS as an overall heading.

How could he then use letters and/or numbers to make clear that items 2-6 belong to that heading? (Write out the contents page again with the letters/numbers added.)

He may do it like this

A. INTRODUCTION

B. ANALYSIS OF COMPLAINTS

    1. Room service

    2. Restaurant service

    3. Bar facilities

    4. Staff/resident relations

    5. Miscellaneous

C. CONCLUSION

D. RECOMMENDATIONS

Notice that he set the numbered points (1-5) closer to the centre of the page. This shows that they are *less* important than the lettered headings, which are closer to the margin. He might also have used the decimal system, e.g.

1. INTRODUCTION

2. ANALYSIS OF COMPLAINTS

    2.1 Room service

    2.2 Restaurant service

    2.3 Bar facilities

    2.4 Staff/resident relations

    2.5 Miscellaneous

3. CONCLUSION

4. RECOMMENDATIONS

Or numbers and small letters, e.g.

1. INTRODUCTION
2. ANALYSIS OF COMPLAINTS

   (a) Room service

   (b) Restaurant service

   (c) Bar facilities

   (d) Staff/resident relations

   (e) Miscellaneous

3. CONCLUSION
4. RECOMMENDATIONS

Had there been *further* sub-divisions to his report then he could have used small numbers as well (e.g. (i), (ii)); or — in the decimal system: a further numbered point — 2.1.1, 2.1.2. Or as in Civil Service reports, each paragraph can be numbered consecutively (1 to 38, or whatever).

Don't worry too much about all these possibilities. Many people, in fact, over-use such devices and succeed only in irritating the reader. Too many numbers and letters can overwhelm and confuse a busy reader. They are necessary only if such numbering actually helps the report writer to organise his material, and to refer the reader easily to another part of the text (e.g. 'See section 2.1' or 'This is covered more fully in A.1'). It should not be necessary to go beyond the simplest system in the kind of short reports most people have to write for most of the time.

In short reports we can use another method of showing the relative importance of the sub-sections — a mixture of capitals, underlining and indentation, e.g.

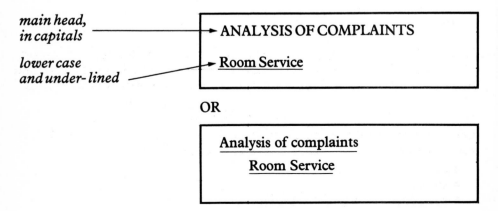

82

If the typewriter permits, it is also possible to use italics. Whatever system you use, it is essential to be consistent, and to check all your headings and sub-headings with this in mind. Consistency is absolutely crucial.

ACTIVITY 2

Consult reports available to you (e.g. at work; in a library). What numbering/lettering systems do they use? How do they use different types and sizes of print to show which headings are important?

In the hotel example we showed that material can sometimes be put at the end of a report as an appendix. This enables the reader who wishes to check details to do so, and other readers to carry straight on. If there is an appendix then the writer should refer the reader to it at the appropriate point, as in the hotel example:

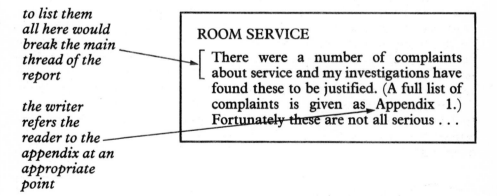

to list them all here would break the main thread of the report

the writer refers the reader to the appendix at an appropriate point

ROOM SERVICE

There were a number of complaints about service and my investigations have found these to be justified. (A full list of complaints is given as Appendix 1.) Fortunately these are not all serious . . .

If appendices are included then they should be listed on the contents page or given a title. They should be placed in the order in which they are mentioned in the text. Thus our hotel contents list should have the appendix added to it:

APPENDIX: COMPLAINTS ABOUT ROOM SERVICE

Glossaries giving the meaning of difficult or technical words, and lists of references, are also sometimes included as appendices, as are

- detailed results and analyses
- statistical data
- specimen forms and documents.

If there are several appendices then these should be numbered (1, 2, 3, etc. or A, B, C, etc.). Notice the appendices in this book.

In longer reports it may be necessary to use footnotes for details (e.g. of sources, for fuller explanations and for qualifications to a point). These can either be placed at the foot of each page (numbered consecutively 1, 2, 3 or a, b, c) or collected together at the end of the report as 'Notes'. Too many footnotes can be confusing, so use them only if absolutely necessary.

If you refer to books or articles then make sure that you include the name of the author (and initials), book title, date, publisher. See Appendix 2 for a way of doing this.

ACTIVITY 3

Consult the reports available to you. Do they use appendices? Do they use footnotes?

It's easy to get lost in all the detail of headings and sub-headings, appendices and the rest. What is important is to remember why some of these features are sometimes necessary and that is — *to make the reader's job easier.* As so often, we return to the reader of the report. If a particular feature will make it easier for your reader to follow your report, then include it. And the importance of the reader leads us to make our final point about layout and presentation: type the report accurately, or write it out very clearly. Your reader's job will be made much harder if your report is tatty, full of mistakes and presented on odd bits and pieces of paper (see Chapter Eleven). We will say something in the next chapter about illustrations.

CHECK YOUR LEARNING

1. In longer reports it is possible that many different sections may be used. Put the following sections into the order in which you would expect them to appear in such reports:

   Conclusion — Title page — Appendix — Main body — Recommendations — Contents page — Introduction

2. The writer of a report feels he must include a list of the names of 60 individuals who provided useful information. Where in the report would you expect to find this list?

3. When we wrote this book we had the following headings for Chapter Two (Terms of reference, titles and introductions):

   What are the 'terms of reference'?; SAQ 1 Thorn 450K; SAQ 2 typing chairs; SAQ 3 Thorn 450K again; SAQ 4 Mrs Stevens; the title of the report; SAQ 5 title for the chairs; the introduction; SAQ 6 Thorn 450K — introduction; SAQ 7 chairs; SAQ 8 chairs; conclusion; activity 1; check your learning; answers to check your learning.

   Lay these out as a contents page for the chapter. Use the conventions you have learnt in this chapter (e.g. letters, numbers and indentation) as you think necessary.

4. Why bother with all these points of presentation? Which of the following statements seem to you the most effective replies to this?
   - (a) To satisfy examiners
   - (b) The reader will expect the report to have a certain shape
   - (c) To make the reader's job easier
   - (d) Lots of things in life are difficult and writing reports is no exception

5. Which of the following points were made in this chapter?
   - (a) short reports should use the decimal numbering system
   - (b) too many numbers or letters in headings can lead to confusion
   - (c) in short reports capitals, indentation and underlining can be used without numbers and letters
   - (d) systems of numbering, etc. should be consistent

Answers to Check Your Learning

1. Title page
   Contents page
   Introduction
   Main body
   Conclusion
   Recommendations
   Appendix

2. In an appendix. If placed in the main text they would be an interruption to the reader.

3.

TERMS OF REFERENCE, TITLES AND INTRODUCTION

(a) **What are the 'terms of reference'?**
   SAQ 1 Thorn 450K
   SAQ 2 Typing chairs
   SAQ 3 Thorn 450K again
   SAQ 4 Mrs Stevens

(b) **The title of the report**
   SAQ 5 Title for the chairs

(c) **The introduction**
   SAQ 6 Thorn 450K — introduction
   SAQ 7 Chairs
   SAQ 8 Chairs

(d) **Conclusion**
   Activity 1

(e) **Check your learning**

(f) **Answers to Check Your Learning**

We have tried to keep this simple, using

- **capitals** for the title of the chapter
- **indentations** to indicate the relative importance of
   section headings
   sub-sections (SAQs)
- **capitals** and **lower case** for section heads
- **letters** for section heads
- a **line** for each of the SAQs

We may have overdone it — the letters for section heads may not be necessary, what do you think?
Compare your own answer with ours. You may have used a different but equally good system.

4. The question does ask you for the *most effective* replies. For us, these are (b) and (c). (a) may be true if you are preparing for an exam which requires you to produce reports. But when you have successfully passed the exam you will need more substantial reasons for continuing to use the conventions of a report. (b) and (c) give the clearest indication of why reports have to be as they are. (d) doesn't seem a very positive view to take!

5. (b), (c) and (d) were made in the chapter. (a) is not made: there is no *one* way which should always be used for *any* report and we suggested that many shorter reports can be just as effective without any system of numbers and letters at all.

Using illustrations

Illustrations can save you and your reader a great deal of time and space. They can condense a large amount of information into a small space. The following **pie chart** quickly and vividly shows that in Britain gas is easily the most popular domestic fuel.

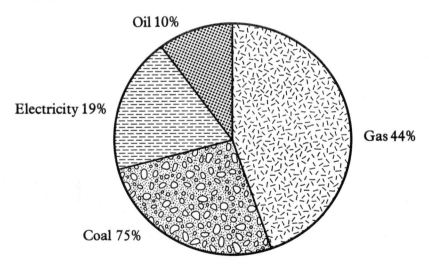

Figure 1 British domestic fuel consumption

Bar charts are another effective way of presenting facts. Here the number or amount is represented by the length of the bar; the width can be varied to suit the space available. The following chart shows the average monthly rainfall totals for a British seaside resort.

Graphs are useful for showing trends, fluctuations or comparisons between quantities:

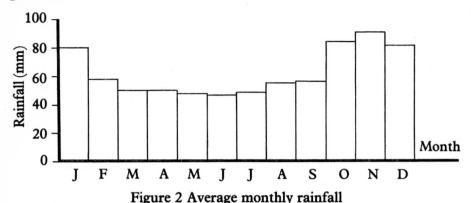

Figure 2 Average monthly rainfall

Some technical reports have to show complex processes or machines by using, for example, labelled diagrams, drawings or flow charts. Other kinds of report may need plans or photographs. You should think about whether the information you have collected can be presented economically and accurately by visual means.

ACTIVITY 1_____

Consult reports available to you. What kinds of illustrations do they use?

If you do use an illustration you must, though, make sure that it really is useful and that its relevance is made clear to the reader. Some reports are full of attractive drawings and other illustrations but they really add very little to what is actually said in words. The following points should help you to use illustrations effectively:

1. Use an illustration *only* if it makes the point more effectively than the written word. (As always, you'll have to think about your reader here: what will communicate your meaning best to that reader?)

2. Position the illustration carefully in the text — as near as possible to the point at which it is mentioned. (Unless you feel that it would be better placed as an appendix — see the discussion of appendices, in the previous chapter.)

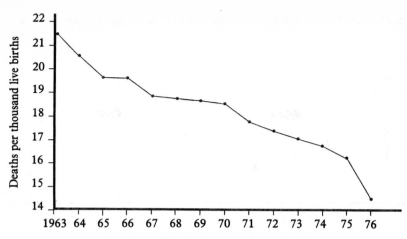

Figure 3   Infant mortality in Britain 1963 to 1976

3. Since you've taken the trouble of putting the illustration in you should discuss it, to integrate it into the text. Ideally, you should introduce it, and then explain its significance.

4. Make the diagram a sensible scale so that it can be read easily. Give details of the scale used.

5. Keep any illustration as simple as you can and in particular don't try to convey too much information on one diagram.

6. Label the parts of a diagram if this will make it clearer.

7. Always caption each illustration so the reader can see at a glance what it shows.

8. If you are using more than one illustration then number them (e.g. Figure 1, Figure 2). You can then make it quite clear to your reader which illustration you are referring to at any given time (e.g. 'Figure 1 showed . . . Figure 2 is . . .')

9. Use illustrations with care: if there are too many they will overwhelm the reader.

ACTIVITY 2_____

Consult a variety of reports and apply the above points to the illustrations.
How effectively do the reports you consult use illustrations?

ACTIVITY 3

Consider your own report(s). Is there scope for illustration? If so, what kind? Make sure that you remember the points made above about using illustrations effectively.

CHECK YOUR LEARNING

1. Below are two lists (a) of report topics and (b) of kinds of illustration. Pair these off to show which topics might need a particular kind of illustration. (Draw lines to connect the relevant items, or write out the lists again if you don't want to mark the book.)

Footpath network in a rural parish	star rating chart
Faults in a printing machine	colour photographs
Good value kettles	map
Selection of flowering shrubs for a park	labelled diagram

Answers to Check Your Learning

1. Footpath network in a rural parish | star rating chart

  Faults in a printing machine | colour photographs

  Good value kettles | map

  Selection of flowering shrubs for a park | labelled diagram

You may have other ideas, for example a labelled diagram for the shrubs, colour photographs for the printing machine. We give the above answer for the following reasons:

- A **map** would be an effective way of showing a footpath network.
- A **star rating chart** (like those in *Which?*) would show how well the various kettles performed.
- The **photographs** would help to show the *colour* of the shrubs, and colour would be an important reason for choice.
- A printing machine is a complex object; a **labelled diagram** would be useful for showing its parts and how they interrelate.

Final presentation of the report

It is difficult to cover all the circumstances you will be in. If, for example, you are working in a large company, you will probably have to hand over your report, handwritten, to a typist. If you are a student then you may have to type the report yourself. Whatever the circumstances, it is very important to make sure that your report looks as clear and attractive as possible — even if the means at your disposal are limited. If you hand the report to a typist then you, the writer, are responsible for ensuring that

- the typist understands exactly how you want it laid out, where diagrams should be placed, how headings are numbered, what should be underlined, how much space to leave, etc.

- handwriting is clear (especially when you are using words likely to be unfamiliar to the typist, or proper names)

- sufficient copies are made and sent to whoever should read them.

It is generally a good idea to ask the typist to use a wide margin on all sides (25mm or more), to leave space between paragraphs and to use double spacing (except, perhaps, for lengthy quotations or for tables). *You* are responsible for the accuracy of the finished work, so leave time for proof-reading. It is also important to give your typist enough time to do the job.

Most reports are typed, photocopied and clipped together for circulation. If your report is to be printed, then even greater care will have to be taken in supervising the final production stages (the BACIE booklet, listed in **Appendix Two**: Further Reading is helpful here). Whatever the shape of your report it is worth thinking out every detail of its final presentation, e.g.

- should it be included in a folder?
  If so, how will it be attached to/within the folder?
- should it be stapled together or attached by paper clip/ bulldog clip?

Each of these methods of 'packaging' the report has advantages and disadvantages and your decision will rest in the end on how the report will be used, on who will be reading it and on whether it will be filed (and if so in what *kind* of filing system).

ASSIGNMENT E

Part 1 You have now practised the key stages involved in report preparation, and are ready to write up your final report. This will be your main piece of work in your last Assignment, and you should remember that in the introduction we suggested a length of 600 to 1800 words.

Write your finished report and send it to your tutor, taking into account any advice you have received. Attend to all the features mentioned in the text so far, not forgetting:

- layout (Chapter Nine)

- illustrations (Chapter Ten)

- final presentation (Chapter Eleven)

Use the checklists in Chapter Twelve as a guide.

Part 2 Write a note to your tutor on

- why you chose the illustrations you used (or why you decided *not* to use any illustrations)

- how you set about checking your work (Chapter Eight and checklists on pp. 97-8)

Part 3 Also write a note on

- where you feel you have made progress during the course

- whether the course met your needs (see your answer to Assignment A)

- aspects of report writing in which you feel you need more practice.

Checklists

Like most other skilled activities, report writing takes time to master. You need to try different approaches to the task and to arrive at a way of working which suits you. You should feel free to adapt the ideas we have suggested in any way that seems helpful to you. In order to improve, you should be self critical and, whenever possible, ask other people what *they* think of your reports. This 'feedback' (from your own assessment of your performance and from the assessments of those who read your reports) gives you an indication of what you need to work at.

ACTIVITY 1_____
Start this process now.
List what you think are the main problems you have when writing reports.
Ask a colleague or tutor what he or she thinks are your main problems.

SAQ 1_____
Below we list problems people may have, together with some suggested solutions. The lists are muddled: which number goes with which letter?

	Problem	**Solutions**	
1	Writes irrelevant conclusions	close check on style, get reader's comments; careful redrafting	A
2	awkward expression	collect material from wider range of sources	B

3	reports are too brief	always check back to (i) terms of reference (ii) title (iii) introduction	C
4	scrappy presentation	leave more time for typing	D

1 goes with C
2 goes with A
3 goes with B
4 goes with D

The solutions suggested may not be the ones which work. For example, 3 may be cured not by using more sources but by better use of 'spray notes' — or by some other activity. You must be prepared to experiment until you find solutions to your problems.

We hope that the checklists which follow will be useful to you in your attempt to produce better reports. The points listed should remind you of what we have put into the chapters. Use the checklists

- to assess your own reports
- to decide where *you* need more help or practice
- to evaluate the reports of others.

Terms of reference (see Chapter Two)

● Are your terms of reference clear? If not, can you get someone to clarify them?
● Are you clear about the *purpose* of your report?
● Are you clear about who will read your report?
  • what does your reader already know about the topic?
  • what does your reader need to know about the topic?
● What *use* will be made of what you write?

Titles and introductions (see Chapter Two)

● Have you written a relevant title?
● Does your introduction
  • refer to the terms of reference (subject, purpose and reader)?
  • refer to any limitations within which you have had to work?
  • give information about the method you used and the plan you have adopted?

Collecting information (see Chapter Three)

- Have you used some method (e.g. spray notes) to record
  - what you already know about the topic
  - what you need to know (your questions)
  - where you might find this information (the answers to your questions)?
- Have you collected information from as many sources as possible/necessary?
- Have you kept a note of the sources of your information?
- Have you used a flexible way of recording the information you get from your sources (e.g. A4 paper or cards)?

Organising the information you have collected (see Chapter Four)

- Is your report presented in clear sections?
- Are these sections placed in a logical sequence?
- Is the report easy to follow?
- Do you 'signpost' your reader enough (e.g. by references to other sections or to appendices)?

Conclusions and recommendations (see Chapter Five)

- Have you written an effective conclusion, i.e. one that
  - is brief and conclusive
  - states the main points arising from the report
  - refers back to the purpose of the report?
- Have you written clear recommendations (either in the conclusion or in a section marked 'Recommendations')?

Writing clear paragraphs (see Chapter Six)

- Does each individual paragraph
  - read as complete in itself?
  - start with a topic sentence which shows what the paragraph is about?
  - group points together to 'fill out' the topic sentence?
  - contain only information relevant to the topic sentence?
- Are the paragraphs in each of your sections linked together?

Writing clearly (see Chapter Seven)

- Do the main ideas emerge clearly from your report?
- Have you considered
  - what your reader knows
  - what your reader needs to know?
- Have you addressed your reader directly and in a suitable tone?
- Are your sentences easy to read?

● Have you checked spelling and punctuation?

● Have you written in the active ('we did') rather than the passive ('it was done')?

Drafting and redrafting (see Chapter Eight)

● Have you made a rough draft?

● Have you checked the structure of your report and amended it as necessary?

● Have you checked the language of your report and amended it as necessary?

● Have you used another person's comments and amended the report as necessary?

● Have you made a final draft?

● Have you proof-read the final draft?

Layout (see Chapter Nine)

● Does your firm/course have an established format for writing reports?
If so, is your report presented in that format?

● Have you used a system for
  • identifying headings (using such devices as underlining, capitals)
  • numbering headings (or giving them letters)?

● If so, is this system
  • necessary
  • consistent?

● Is the contents page accurate?

● Are references to all sections/appendices/illustrations accurate?

● Is your report typed or clearly written?

Illustrations (see Chapter Ten)

● Have you used illustrations where these are necessary?

● Have you made clear to the reader the relevance of these illustrations?

● Are the illustrations positioned effectively?

● Is each illustration
  • clearly drawn
  • captioned
  • numbered
  • referred to in the text?

● Have unnecessary details been cut out?

Final presentation (see Chapter Eleven)

● Have you given the typist clear instructions?

● In what form, and how, will the report be distributed?

● Have you allowed enough time for these final stages?

Appendix one: Scientific and technical reports

You must be prepared to adapt the format you use for reports; each organisation has its own requirements. We have already mentioned the kinds of adjustment you may need to make and said that you should consult any instructions your firm/college provides on format. Sometimes, for example, recommendations are stated after each section in the main text, as well as in a separate section at the end; sometimes reports *begin* with a summary. Short 'summary' sections can be included along the way, in a substantial report. These adjustments can be easily made; your job is to find out about any such requirements *well in advance*, so you can prepare your report accordingly.

But students taking technical and science courses in universities and other such institutions will have to make more significant adjustments when writing reports on experimental work. In this case formats similar to the following are customary:

Summary (also called **Abstract** or **Synopsis**)
This is a brief statement of the *whole* report. It is wise to leave this until last. Write the report and *then* write the summary. Include brief details of
- why you decided to carry out the experiment
- what you found
- the significance of what you found.

Introduction
The same rules apply as for other reports — a careful statement of purpose and a mention of any limitations. (Method, though, is left to the *next* section.)

Method
The method used is of special importance in experimental work. Those reading your report will want to evaluate the method you have chosen. They need to know about it in detail. You would refer to such things as the apparatus you used and the procedure you adopted.

Results
This is similar to the conclusions section in other reports. You explain, carefully, what happened.

Discussion
In this section you discuss the significance of your results, comparing them

with the results of other scientists. You *interpret* your results.

Appendices can also be added if necessary.

Appendix two: Further reading

Many books and pamphlets have been published on report writing. We consulted about 15 when preparing this text. Unfortunately, few of them are of any great use. The best one we found is:

Business Research and Report Writing by Robert L. Shurter, J. Peter Williamson and Wayne G. Broehl Jr. (published by McGraw-Hill, 1965).

This deals with some of the topics in this book but in more detail (e.g. points of grammar, how to construct a logical argument, statistics, illustrations). Even this book has its limitations: it is now rather dated; it is based on American experience and it relates specifically to business. But it is useful if you feel you need a more advanced treatment of the subject of report writing.

A Guide to Report Writing by Judith Vidal-Hall (published by The Industrial Society, 1977) is a short guide which packs a great deal of useful advice into 30 pages.

100% Report Writing by R. A. Ward (published by R. and H. Ward, Patches, Wellington Ave., Virginia Water, Surrey, 1977) is a useful short aid. (24pp., 70p at 1981 prices)

Report Writing (published by BACIE, 1977) is very authoritative but expensive (£2.60 for 24pp., at 1981 prices). It has useful appendices, including one on printers' alterations.

Report Writing for Management by William J. Gallagher (published by Addison-Wesley 1968) is the most comprehensive and advanced manual on report writing in business yet seen.

How to Write Reports by John Mitchell (published by Fontana, revised edition 1981) is a useful general guide, very detailed, with a helpful section on collecting material.

For further advice on writing and studying generally
The following NEC courses are helpful:
- *How to Write Essays* breaks down the task of writing an essay into manageable parts.
- *Learning to Study* helps you decide whether you are suited to studying and how you will study best.
- *How to Study Effectively* gives practical information on study skills for adult students.
- *Writing* covers types of writing needed for study, note-taking, and essay writing.

Reference books
Collins Concise English Dictionary or the *Concise Oxford Dictionary* are both excellent.

Roget's Thesaurus (available in Penguin) can help you to pinpoint the right word, or to find alternative words.

Appendix three: Sequence for items in a report

- Title page (title, sub-title (if necessary), date, name of writer, circulation list)
- Summary (abstract or synopsis)
- Contents list (may also be shown on title page or not shown at all, depending on the length of the report)
- Introduction
- Main text
- Conclusion
- Recommendations
- Appendices

(Not all these features need appear in every report.)

COURSE COMMENTS

We would be interested to hear your reactions to this course. Send your comments to The Courses Editor, NEC, 18 Brooklands Avenue, Cambridge CB2 2HN.

Name (Mr, Mrs or Ms) ....

Student Number ....

Address ....

....

....

Report Writing ED 26